Ragan's poetry echoes [...] u-
alize his hope for the future. He has lived his life with [...] .ne
grief. All three feelings share the positives of his book. I am delighted to
welcome you to his story, and pleased to be known as his friend.

—Jeannette Clift George
Founder and Artistic Director
A.D. Players Theater

Having known Ragan and his work for many years, I am not surprised by this honest confession of raw grief. The reaction to death for many people of faith is an embarrassment that is to be covered by holy emotions and spiritual shoulds. This collection of poems is like the lancing of festering, aching wounds in response to dismissive invitations to accept that "time will heal the hurt." Recognizing that in all of life and especially in the shadow experience of "waiting for the fog to part," we learn "eternity's lessons." *Holy Ghosts* frees us to feel and keep on feeling. It is not a curse to feel; it is a curse to miss the opportunity to move from the present to the eternal, and to reject the idea there has "to be ignorance in order for faith to come into play."

—Bill Heston
Executive Pastor, First Presbyterian Church, Houston

I am so glad the world will finally know what I've known for over 30 years. Ragan Courtney is a true poet. Enjoy!

—Mark Lowry
Singer, Songwriter, and Comedian

Ragan Courtney's vulnerability is so real in these poems that you can almost hear his voice in the vivid imagery. Sometimes gently and sometimes with force, he coaxes light out of the darkness of loss and sorrow. With each poem he helps us yield our fears of death and dying bit by bit, calling us to "believe a bit more, sing a bit louder and pray a bit deeper." It is a glad irony that he shows us another way to celebrate life and all of its mysteries. I was profoundly affected by the raw and rich beauty of *Holy Ghosts*.

—Jeanie Miley
Author of Fierce Love *and* Meeting Jesus Today

Smyth & Helwys Publishing, Inc.
6316 Peake Road
Macon, Georgia 31210-3960
1-800-747-3016
©2016 by Ragan Courtney
All rights reserved.

Library of Congress Cataloging-in-Publication Data

Names: Courtney, Ragan, author.
Title: Holy ghosts / by Ragan Courtney.
Description: Macon, GA : Smyth & Helwys Publishing, 2016.
Identifiers: LCCN 2016003387 | ISBN 9781573128711 (paperback : alk. paper)
Classification: LCC PS3553.O862 A6 2016 | DDC 811/.54--dc23
LC record available at http://lccn.loc.gov/2016003387

Disclaimer of Liability: With respect to statements of opinion or fact available in this work of nonfiction, Smyth & Helwys Publishing Inc. nor any of its employees, makes any warranty, express or implied, or assumes any legal liability or responsibility for the accuracy or completeness of any information disclosed, or represents that its use would not infringe privately-owned rights.

HOLY GHOSTS

RAGAN COURTNEY

Deanie,
Thanks for your help you came to my "aid."
Celebrate Life!
Ragan Courtney

Also by Ragan Courtney

Poems

Meditations for the Suddenly Single

The Wind I Soar On

Death Has Set My Mind on Fire

Three Voices

And so as kinsmen met a-night,
We talked between the rooms . . .
—Emily Dickinson

This book is dedicated to
Clarence Andrew Chapman, Eddie Gay,
Sarah Ann Williamson, Sybil Courtney,
Francis Courtney, Patience Octavia Courtney,
William F. Courtney, Kent Chapman,
Emma Brumfield Chapman, Kenneth Courtney,
Raymond Brown, Virginia Clawson,
Thomas W. Clawson, Bill James, and Buryl Red

And in memory of Don Nixon

Contents

Preface	xi
Death Has Set My Mind on Fire	1
Sybil's Song	2
When Death Comes to Call	3
Time Heals?	5
Faith Locked	7
Before She Went to Live with Light	8
Wraiths Seem Real	9
R.I.P.	10
Spring Is Sweet	11
Introduction into Grief	12
On Psalm 23	19
Deadly News (For Raymond)	20
Dry Bones	23
Night Spangle	26
Hotel Ghost	27
Insight	28
Tracks on His Soul (thoughts on a young man's suicide)	29
The Odyssey	31
A Grave for a Dove (For Dr. Allen Reasons)	33
Scattered Leaves	35
My Dog Died	36
On the Occasion of Duke's Death	38
To Dwight	40
Mayan Dream	42
Sunset	44
Whispering Hope	45
Beginning Again	47
Sun Baptized	48
I Have Witnessed	51
Grotesque Buoys	52
They Gathered Like Country Guests	54
Forty Years Ago	55

Like a Wilted Dandelion	57
Forgive Me for Staring	58
And a Time to Die	59
Heart Song	60
Grief Resurfacing	61
It Is Easter Again	63
Eternal Lullaby	66
I Saw God Today	67
In the Tomb	70
Looking Out	72
What's the Word?	74
Bonhoeffer's Grave	76
Buchenwald	78
Truth Arrived	80
It's a Funeral Day	82
Yesterday's Pains	83
More Questions	84
Visitation	86
Where Are You Wandering?	87
And the Darkness Can Never Conquer	88
Resurrection Morning	89
Maya Angelou	92
One Year Later (Or a Lifetime)	93
Mother Emanuel Church	94
Last Will and Testament	96
The Death of the Good Reverend	98
Hope Eternal	100

Preface

I was told that my great-grandfather, Clarence Andrew Chapman, was a political ally of Huey P. Long, infamous governor of Louisiana. My antecedent was known in his community as Boss Chapman, and I only knew him as Grandpa Boss until I started this preface and uncovered his complete name. Governor Long would stop by my great-grandfather Boss Chapman's house and they would talk politics there in the poverty-ridden, rural, congressional district of St. Helena Parish, not far from Kedron Baptist Church.

My great-grandfather was well known as a colorful character who reared his siblings after the premature deaths of their parents in the late 1800s. He was the oldest child, and as a young man he learned about lumber and how to look across acres of timber and give a good estimate of how much money could be made from the old growth covering the land. He also kept a passel of "chaps"—as he called his brothers and sisters—fed and clothed.

Years later, as an adult, he was patriarch of what inevitably turned out to be a painfully dysfunctional family. He seemed to be the personification of Tennessee Williams's character Big Daddy from *Cat on a Hot Tin Roof*. In his seventies as he was running for state office, a big first step before running for governor of Louisiana, he got sick with cancer, and to his family, it was as though the Creator God, the heavenly Father himself were waning. I was five years old, and I remember my mother crying at the news of his illness and later sobbing when he died. Death was a visitor whom I was ever aware of from that young age forward as being just outside the door.

I have witnessed many deaths, from great-grandparents to grandparents to parents to friends. I was always taught not to fear death, so I would give it a cursory nod and look the other way and continue to live in a culture where, if denial were not the only way to cope with the inevitability of death, then stories of streets of gold and eternal mansions certainly were. The visions of golden streets have ultimately failed to block my fear of the unknown, however, even when wrapped in folds of gospel harmonies higher and thicker than Grandma's patchwork quilts.

When I had a massive heart attack from which I was revived even after my heart stopped for a few minutes, I got another impression of death that changed my perspective. As I hovered in the upper corner of the operating room at ceiling height and looked down at the doctors compressing my chest, I thought to myself, "This does *not* look good! But at least I am still thinking." I did not address the being I sensed to my left as surely as I sense the keys under my fingers as I write this, but I knew that I was not alone. And, as I said, I knew I was continuing to think, even joking as I observed my limp body on the bed below. I distinctly remember thinking, "Well, if I'm dead, I'll be with God and my family members who have already gone on. If I'm not dead, I'll continue to be with my wife and children. I guess I've got a win-win situation here. Because I'm still thinking!" I remember being unafraid then, and I remain unafraid to this day.

Waking up, I knew I had seen no white lights, tunnels, Jesus, or either of my parents, who had preceded me in death, but I was absolutely assured that I had continued to *be* during the time of my cardiac arrest, my brief death. Stories I have read about glorious days of living in heaven with Jesus as my next-door neighbor and experiencing bliss beyond the ability to express have puzzled me profoundly. I don't think the storytellers are lying, but why didn't God have Lazarus write us a little testimonial about what heaven is like? He could have slipped such stories into the Bible right before John's book about his revelation. Somehow, death is still part of the great mystery that is God. We know very little about it.

Writing about death could be construed morbid, but I don't think that is why I did it. This ever-present phantom is a constant companion. Those with enough awareness realize that death is inevitable. Many have experienced grief firsthand with the death of a friend or family member. In the first grade, my neighborhood playmate, Eddie, a child of six, suddenly sickened and died in a matter of days. I could not grasp it; for years afterward, when I went into a dark schoolroom, hallway, empty church—any place where I was alone in the dark—I felt that Eddie was there. I always felt a shiver of the unknown that I thought was fear. At fourteen, Sara Ann, another neighbor, was accidentally burned to death. My childhood was haunted by specters and ghosts. They seemed as real as the eternal humidity that lightly swathed our fragile faith with damp doubts about the happy endings and mansions just over the hilltop.

My mother died at forty-eight years of age. The loss was stunning. Her dying did not engender more fear of death; in fact, as she suffered and died, she showed me that death was nothing to fear. During those days, well-meaning friends often said to me that we should not grieve as those without hope. I would nod and offer a sanctimonious smile, but what I heard was that if you were a good Christian, you would celebrate a saved soul's release and not grieve. That is not healthy. Grief is part of recovering from the loss of someone.

I find that death is a part of living. I wanted to be open and honest as I talked about this part of our journey as mortals. Sages, prophets, sibyls—even saviors—speak of immortality to us. As I noted earlier, we did not get scriptural details from Lazarus, Jarius's daughter, the widow of Nain's son, or Jesus when they came back from death and walked among us. I find this interesting.

I have observed that there are those who have passed, gone on, slipped past this mortal coil, passed over, passed away, left, died—to paraphrase Monty Python—who still affect our lives. They come as dreams, memories, fleeting thoughts, haunting and hurting memories, or regrets. Sometimes we weep for what is no more, sometimes we laugh at the delight of a particular memory, sometimes we wail because the pain of separation can't be expressed any other way. When the dead come to mind, they are like holy ghosts, as real as hope or faith, as tangible as trust and love. This book is a collection of questions, memories, and loves that continue to live with me, in me, and through me.

I have written these words on a subject that is mysterious and generally considered depressing. I can't imagine a long line of people waiting at a bookstore for copies of a book dealing with the sobering subject of death. Also, many agents and publishers have assured me that poetry is neither popular nor profitable. Make the subject of your poetry *death*, and you will learn how short those bookstore lines can be. Yet death is a topic that moves us all one way or the other. Here are the remembrances of family and friends who have died and still haunt my thoughts. Here is displayed the basis of my personal faith that encompasses the story of a man who rose from the dead and showed all who would see that death is not the end. Life is. Period. I hope these poems will help readers not to feel fear as they stand in a dark schoolroom, hallway, and empty church, waiting for the light to come on.

Note: Some of these poems were previously printed by Convention Press, Broadman Publishers, Triune Music, and Zondervan Publishers.

Death Has Set My Mind on Fire

Death has set my mind on fire.
He has stirred my brain with his
Long, black poker
Taken dying thoughts, buried deep,
And pulled them into the air.
They explode into flame,
Burn up my remembrances
And leave me alone in ashes.
Job, what do you do with ashes?

Sybil's Song

You said you had learned something
And friends dropped by to see
What exotic news there could possibly be,
Sybil, sage-colored sage.
In your quick glimpses over there,
Tell us, what did you see?
Help us solve the mystery,
Frail, trembling Sybil.
Tell us what color, please, is eternity?
Is it white or green or bright sky blue?
Is light all there is?
Is everything new,
Or do you feel you've been there before?
Why are you silent? There must be more you can say.
Can you hear me?
Sybil, Sybil, must you go away?
I had hoped to finally learn the answer today.

When Death Comes to Call

When death comes to call
His pale card is left on a table in the foyer,
And he is invited into the living room,
An expected,
If not always welcomed guest
Dressed in his fine, white summer suit.
Life is offered to us like a neat, crust-less cucumber sandwich
On a sterling-silver serving tray,
And we ingest it.
Some gobble it down,
Like gluttons licking their fingers.
Others nibble at the edges
Like shy spinsters
Still wearing white, lace gloves.
In either case, before we know it,
It is consumed.
Death takes the tray from us
And blows the crumbs into the air.
They fall like mournful confetti on the Oriental rug—
Tiny remembrances of a feast that was all too brief—
Only to be hastily swept from plush carpet
Designed to absorb the sounds of shuffling feet
Inching past a funeral pall.
We grieve not the brevity of the meal.
We are distressed at the incompleteness of it.

There was so much more that we intended
To do,
To see,
To learn,
To taste.
And that is when Death, gracious as a friend,
We hope,
Extends an invitation
To another feast,
One that nurtures with elements more eternal.
Wine flows and bread is broken,
And the servant host
Dines with us as he welcomes us home.

But we do not want you to be uninformed, brethren, about those who are asleep, that you may not grieve, as do the rest who have no hope. For if we believe that Jesus died and rose again, even so God will bring with Him those who have fallen asleep in Jesus.

THESSALONIANS 4:13-14

Time Heals?

Time will heal the hurt
They said.
Soon you will not think of her as
Dead—
Rather gone away
(What a stupid thing to say.)
Time has proved a faulty physician.
In unsuspecting moments I perceive
My bereft condition,
And wish my memory could be as constant
As Old Faithful
And erupt at planned intervals
Hot grief.
At least I would be prepared.
Instead, some inner broken clock
Sets off my erratic geyser
And sweet memories slide down my face.
For instance:
When flying high above clouds,
I am reminded of biscuit dough,

Then her hands in the dough,
Then her hands,
Then her.
And I know,
I know
Time can never heal Now's hurts
And Now? . . .
Now lasts forever.

Faith Locked

Mother—
Such a holy loss
Cancer—
Such an ugly cross
Jesus—
Since you paid the cost
To set her free,
Help me understand
The enormity
Of Life
When the solemnity
Of Death
Keeps my faith locked
In an iron casket
As gray and heavy
As Mama's
Old Dutch oven.

Before She Went to Live with Light

Before she went to live with light,
Her shadow passed over me,
And I learned.
In the coolness of the shade
She made
I grew.
Now I stand
In the glare of the departure
Learning eternity's lessons.

Wraiths Seem Real

Wraiths seem real.
I can see their shadows
And I fear
They can torture and kill.
They slink behind a stone,
Around a bend,
Beyond my sight.
They drink the night
And spit out the stars.
Their home is in the Valley of the Shadow.
I dare not go there alone.
I need a song
Or a psalm
To keep me calm,
To illuminate my way
Down the well-worn path
Eroded by the unending line of predecessors
Who have gladly testified
Those specters are no more real
Than fear,
Or lies.

R.I.P.

One day you realize—
Your soul filled with sighs and whys—
That it never could be.
What you thought should be
Wouldn't be.
Your dreams were only dreams
No more than shimmering rainbows.
And so your hopes of happiness
Fade
Like glimmering pots
Brimming with ephemeral gold.

Spring Is Sweet

Spring is sweet,
But buds are too delicate, too petite.
Full summer leaves give more shade,
Are more open to the wind.
They bend, and sigh and play
In a coquettish way.
Then shivering with each lingering autumnal touch,
Unaware of Frost
Until he kisses their openness and they blush
And faint in a crimson flurry,
Leaving their fullness in too much of a hurry.
Having a solitary encounter,
They faint, falling in celebration
Of an ecstatic consequence
Of a longing
For just one more touch.

As he had come naked from his mother's womb, so will he return as he came. He will take nothing from the fruit of his labor that he can carry in his hand.

ECCLESIASTES 5:15

Introduction into Grief

When I watch the leaves
Sear,
Color,
And fall,
I think of
Mother.
As a child I was called
Mama's boy in ridicule—
Now it is a noble title,
Mama's Boy.
Her illness began in the fall,
Clung to her the next fall;
And destroyed her four days after
Christmas.
Her skin turned from a jaundiced shade
To an old gold,
And her face withered like oak leaves.
Her ample figure wasted.
She wrinkled, looking twice her forty-eight
Years.
Such a momentous occasion,

My mother's death,
I watched her final breath,
Saw her beautiful little finger
Curve
Then freeze
As though she were having
A morning cup of dreams with angels.
I watched my father
Straighten her hand,
Kiss her forehead,
Gently close her eyes,
Place her fragile head straight on the
Pillow
And bend his own in grief.
I looked from him
Down to her still form.
The pulse that I had watched
And counted for days
Had been totaled.
The final figure was not enough.
Not enough!
The beat had stopped
And the rhythm took
On eternal proportions.
She was gone.
I felt no need to embrace
Her body.
As I felt her presence leave,

I lost all sense of composure.

Anguish

Erupted

Flooding my being

With foreign emotions.

Hot,

Seething,

Red

Grief.

Why?

God, why?

My mother gone.

DEAD.

Motherless.

This is what's happening now . . .

NOW

I am standing beside

My mother's body.

God.

God!

GGGOOOOOODDD!

I can't bear this pain.

I'm going under.

I'm going to scream.

Daddy, what can we do?

Don't cry; I love you.

Let's run.

Help me.

Pain.
Red.
I hurt.
I see death
I am afraid . . .

Toward the end she slept
For longer and longer periods.
She slept—
Hands folded—
Like a little girl in prayer.
I brushed her hair.
And waited with the others.
She was covered with a white sheet
In a white room,
In a white building,
In a white society.
Miss Sybil—
White Southern lady
Asleep.
Dreaming of what?
What thoughts flickered
Through her mind?
Did she see past her white world
To a world of brilliant color,
And past color
To pure light?
Time was illuminated

By the ultraviolet light
That shines during
Life-and-death
Transitions.
No longer did people speak
Of this miracle
Or that healing.
Instead, they shook their heads, saying,
"We shouldn't
Question God."
I did. I do.
Why?
WHY?
Why pain, operations,
Endless needles, pumps,
Nausea?
Platitudes and pat answers don't
Work when you know them all.
I prayed.
I begged.
I remembered
Her prayer.
The day before we took her
Back to the hospital.
It was simple and polite and honest.
It was a victorious example
Of an unquenchable faith.
I remembered holding her soft, dry hand

As we prayed together.

She addressed her Creator

With polite respect and said,

"Our most gracious heavenly Father,

Thank you for life . . .

Thank you for the young people . . ."

(She meant me.)

"Thank you for the pain,

I've learned so much through it . . .

And most of all,

Thank you for Jesus . . .

Amen."

Not one request.

Not one,

"God, please . . ."

Only gratitude.

She was dying,

In pain,

Sick,

And she said,

"Thank you."

Because she believed:

Jesus loved her,

He went to prepare a place for her,

He would take her to himself

In a new home,

New mansion,

New dimension.

She was able to say,
"And most of all, thank you for Jesus . . ."
Most of all, thank you for Jesus.
And, Jesus, thank you
For Mama.

On Psalm 23

Lord, I walked to the edge
Of the valley with her.
I could go no further.
She seemed so small and frail,
Dwarfed by the towering walls of the chasm
Rising before her.
I saw her flinch from her first spasm of fear.
Each raw pillar of stone grew,
Crowned with grotesque gargoyles
Towering over her frailty,
Vomiting fear and doubt about
What lay ahead
For the dead.
But she and I seemed to notice
At the same time
The secret that only those who enter
The forlorn Valley of the Shadow learn:
To have a shadow
There must be a directional source of light.
She kept walking
Toward that light.
The closer she got,
The larger her shadow became,
Until that was all I could see of her.

Deadly News
(For Raymond)

The news came crawling
Like dreaded, deadly spiders into my ear,
Spewing their gossip like a lethal poison.
It was your name they whispered,
Your name now linked forever with a dreaded disease.
Your name that had blinked in our dreams in large Broadway marquee
letters
Like advertisements to all the ambitions we would realize
During our callow days of infinite possibilities.
Now, we have only finite things to contemplate like:
Estates, wills, a memorial service.
A memorial to you
Who clung with such tenacity to people
Hoping to find approval,
Hoping to find acceptance,
Hoping to find love.
Oh, I understood your yearnings for fame,
For belonging.
I understood your need that sent you homing
Back to Oklahoma looking for permission to be
True to who you really were.
And you really were humorous, witty and remarkable.
You heard music—original or derivative—
It did not matter,

It was beautiful,

And it sang of truth

Like nothing else in your life.

Why did you listen to the lies from others

About who you were?

Could you not hear in my voice

The awe you inspire?

Could you not believe

The one who was the "Portal of your Art"?

Could you not see and hear it in your own songs?

You were such an accepting friend to so many—

Especially to me—

But such a bad friend to yourself.

When the grim news arrived,

Tears and speechless silences punctuated our hushed conversation

That seemed the opening measure of the prelude to your requiem,

A requiem you wrote long ago.

Poor artist, time is brief,

Talent aborted,

Love misspent on those who

Mostly returned insensibility and judgment

For your uniqueness.

Now we both must take what is offered us

And make what we can from it

As we add this unknown ingredient

To all the facets that have made up our friendship.

Is there one last thing that Death can help us compose

As he gives you your personal map revealing

The particular path you are to take?
It is not a broad path, friend.
It is winding and narrow, not straight.
It is dark and full of uncertainties.
It is steep and scary
And solitary.
You must go it alone.
I would go with you, honest to God,
But that is impossible.
Only the one in whom you have trusted can travel with you,
And he is an invisible companion,
But I have been assured that he is there,
Providence sustaining even now.
Is he?
You tell me—
Tell us.
Is he there with you as you walk through the valley of the shadow
To home?

Dry Bones

We are told that there was nothing, and then God spoke and there was everything.
Hard to grasp, but who can refute it?
God created
Something from nothing,
Everything from nothing!
How?
Who can say?
But the sky is blue,
The sun is warm,
Birds sing,
And ants scurry,
Dogs run through the fields in a hurry,
Cats loll,
The moon is cool.
Like an isolated pearl in a dark sea,
It reflects light
And keeps the night from being so dark.
And people populate the planet
Love, union and birth—
Sometimes union and no birth,
And other times birth and no love,
But there is always death.
"Are we born simply to die?" we cry,
As the graves and tombs slowly fill,

As wars, disease, and time inevitably kill.
And can all those bones—
Scattered across the valley floors
Folded neatly into boxes,
Piled up in catacombs,
Burned to ashes in crematoria—
with a spoken prophetic word, rise again,
Bone to sinew to muscle to skin?
When the breath of the spoken word
Calls them, they will answer
Because the same voice that commanded
Light to be
Looks at those atoms—
His diminutive tools—
And rearranges them as he pleases.
And they are going to walk around.
Them bones, them bones,
Them dry bones!
So here we are
Sitting in neat rows
Orderly, ritually doing church.
Some nap, some pray,
Some bide their time until they can escape the boring neatness of
Organized religion.
And while we sit, time passes.
The sanctuary becomes a tomb.
The pews, rows of coffins
Where everybody looks so nice and natural

And dead.

Time strips the flesh from the bones,

Exposing what we have tried to deny and hide all the days of our lives.

Are we all alike down deep,

The pious, the reprobate

The arrogant, the meek

The saint, the sinner

The doer, the thinker

The lover, the hater

The glutton, the famished

The chaste, the philanderer

All dried up and dead from ordinary orthodoxy,

Routine, religious ritual?

Could it be that there is something beyond death and the grave?

Could it be that we are the very ones he came dying to save?

Could it be that he would choose to warm our brittle bones?

Could it be that in him we finally find our home?

Night Spangle

Night, you spangle the vault of heaven
With stars burned crisp.
Poisonous, malignant,
Sooty, soiled vapors
Ascend from the tortured bowels of the earth
That you deprive of light.
You enfold the earth in the shadow of dark, suffocating wings,
Its fragile crust crumbling into dust
With your death grip.
Who can wield the sliver of light
That will pierce Night to her secret, black heart,
Causing inky emotions to leak
From her breast
Like death,
Reducing her goddess role to one of mere astronomy?

Hotel Ghost

In between ornate arches,
Underneath carved ceilings,
Forgotten memories sit demurely,
Whispering in an unknown tongue
Purple prose,
Remembering days
Before their fragile lives had faded.
Like pressed roses in dusty Bibles
They have been crushed between the years
And forgotten.
Then
She enters again.
The train of her dress
Is silent on the marble stairs.
No one sees her glide through
The grand lobby,
No one hears her laugh and call
To forgotten beaus.
No one sees her float through
The closed etched-glass doors
And whirl away
To an eternal waltz,
Leaving in her wake
The faint scent of
Bruised gardenias.

Insight

Half waking
I thought I caught a glimpse of it—
That other world.
It was clearer than this reality,
Brighter, sharper.
And the sighting concerned me lest it be a
Premonition of my immediate departure.
I saw trees shading a tranquil lake
Maxfield Parrish-blue,
And light, more sparkling and scintillating than mere reflection.
There is no denying that it seemed more real there than here
(Or I seemed less real here than there.)
What was it I saw?
Hereafter?
Paradise?
I can't say, but it gave me pause
To think about what is real
And what is illusion.
Hope is the one thing that maintains us
As we continue to move
Inexorably towards the long-awaited conclusion!

Tracks on His Soul
(thoughts on a young man's suicide)

There were no tracks on your arms.
They hung by your side alabaster smooth,
Young
With the potential for heroic strength.
They were used mostly as levers to lift countless brews
Cocktails,
Rotgut,
Bathtub gin,
Moonshine—
Legal opiate of the disenfranchised,
Sacrament for the cannibalistic communion where you eat your own heart.
"This is my body broken . . ."
Rituals spoken
About cheap wine, a token
Of all the blood spilt
By countless tortured people
Kicked in the teeth and tossed away, left beside the road
Waiting for the Good Samaritan.
The tracks are on your soul,
Invisible to the ignorant.
Only the initiated see where ulcerated wounds testify
To all attempts at self-medication.
Addictions stab like rusty, crusty needles

Making too many punctures
Trying to dull too many years of pain
Sending poison like red spider webs
Up white arms of your listless soul
Ensnaring your brain like a sick, gray thing in a net.
And the night comes when there is no hope of ever stopping the pain.
It sears like ancient fires spewed from the belly of great roaring coal-fed engines.
Hell is living one more day, one more moment in torment.
Finally, that December night, running in the cold night air,
Arms waving frantically to signal that you are here waving good-bye—
Your agony brings you to the train track.
A rail becomes your pillow,
Your arms lay at your side resigned to never move
As the Missouri Pacific roars by like an avalanche of steel
Cleaving you
Leaving final tracks on your alabaster arms.
Swing low, sweet chariot, coming for to carry you home.

The Odyssey

To set out in such a frail craft seems lunacy.
Whose idea was it anyway?
From this perspective the water is dark, deep, and definitely cold.
How can I possibly hope to traverse that wet expanse?
I cannot walk on water like Jesus did.
I cannot part it like Moses did.
There is no specter in a Grecian death mask
To ferry me across the River Styx.
I feel no fear, only perplexing amazement
That it should be ordained that I must travel this course,
That the departure would be so imminent.
Why am I here at this timeless shore
Looking at such a still sea
With no discernible shore for a destination?

From this vantage point,
I see only a misty distance.
Could that mist hide a cloud of witnesses?
Could the hint of parents around my bed days ago
Be a foreshadowing of a traveling companion?
Are there only questions?
Does there have to be ignorance in order for faith to come into play?
I am not particularly frightened at this ceaseless seashore,
Only lonely and a bit sad.
I keep looking into the black water and the gray mist,

Waiting for the fog to part like a heavy moist curtain
And reveal him walking across the waters smiling,
Arms outstretched to embrace me,
Then following,
The evidence of things not seen.

A Grave for a Dove
(For Dr. Allen Reasons)

With a thud the bird hit the church window.
One moment it was skimming through the humid Houston air
When without warning
There was interposed to its journey
A large, invisible glass plate
Stopping the bird abruptly in mid-flight.
The noise caused us to turn, look out of the window
And there lying on the grass, quivering
Was a creature who two seconds ago was darting about the heavens
Full of life.
My friend and I looked at one another
In bewilderment.
Surely he will come to.
He is merely stunned, we both agreed.
Did not the Bible speak of God knowing when the sparrow falls?
Or was God aware that
The creature in question was not a sparrow,
Rather a dove,
A gentle, muted gray bird
With a woeful, mournful, song
As sad as twilight?
I rushed outdoors
And picked up the mortally wounded mourner.
It lay in my hand like a whisper.

Its shape was not unlike a heart
With its wings folded
And it's neck too frightfully limber.
One drop of blood ran down its beak
Falling to the verdant yard,
A ruby exhibited on green velvet.
What does one do with fresh death?
My friend walked to a flowerbed
Exploding with colorful, jeweled blossoms,
Scratched out a grave for a dove,
And we—gently covering the innocent creature with warm earth—
Listened to its mate call and call
And call.

Scattered Leaves

Scattered leaves on the walk
Like rusty, broken toys
Autumn discarded
Eddy around rag doll men
All their joys and dreams thwarted,
Except for the joy in the amber fluid swirling.
In their corn husk heads memories stop,
And in the rain they don't feel cold,
Merely old.
While their souls
Hibernate in anticipation of an
Eternal winter.

For the fate of the sons of men and the fate of beasts is the same. As one dies so dies the other; indeed, they all have the same breath and there is no advantage for man over beast, for all is vanity. All go to the same place. All came from the dust and all return to the dust.

ECCLESIASTES 3:19-20

My Dog Died

My dog died today.
Worms.
Didn't know until too late.
They got in him and drank up all his blood.
His gums was white.
He was terrible skinny—
Ate a lot, though
Until he was too weak to chew.
Then he just lay there…
Then we knew.
Called a veterinarian.
Doctor said he was dying—
Any fool could see that.
Said he would put him to sleep—
He meant kill him.
Papa said, OK.
Mama asked how long before
The shot took effect.
Doctors said almost immediately—
Wasn't no almost to it.

He died right then and there
In the shadow of the Ford.
His eyes was open
Even after he died.
I could tell he was dead
Because all the flies walked on his eyes
And he didn't blink.
Clyde hit him with a long, heavy wire
To make sure he was dead.
He flopped, then was still.
Mama told him to stop that.
I cried.
We didn't have no funeral
Didn't seem right to play-like
When death was so real.

On the Occasion of Duke's Death

It is a landmark day today.
Jews and Palestinians fight,
Politicians bicker like blackbirds trying to make room
On a telephone wire,
And Duke, the Dog of Dogs, died too soon.
He used to walk over to the table
Where folks were dining
His eyes nearly table height.
He would silently, reverently ask—without whining—
To participate in the communal meal.
One brow would lift, then the other
And someone—usually a visitor—
Would place a scrap of food on his great pink tongue
Like communion wafer.
With a gulp it was gone!
"Duke!" his master would call, correcting him—
And the guest—
For begging as though he were a recalcitrant child.
Then Duke would turn with dignity and walk away,
Plop on the cool tile floor,
His golden eyes filled with merriment.
Today his other Master called him
To a new family table where St. Francis offers him
A veritable feast of delicious scraps
Like he does to all creatures that have been redeemed

By the love of their earthly masters.

Duke's golden eyes are now filled with wonder.

To Dwight

I heard your departure was imminent
When it was already, in truth, a fact.
For the life of me
I can't imagine why you should have left so soon.
"A matter of days," your wife said.
You were confined to your bed,
Sons by your head, I hope.
Memories of things past
Boiling in your fevered brain,
Releasing innocuous vapors,
Distilling your life to its condensed essence:
Redeemed child,
Elegant gentleman,
Creative artist,
Loving father,
Determined husband . . .

I remember that frigid winter night—
Years ago—
When we sat erect in Windsor chairs
Sipping port
(Or was it hot tea?)
Anyway, it felt terribly English to me.
There, comparing life wounds,
We surprised each other by weeping together—

An intimacy that startled us both
Like a hot cinder that exploded from the dying fire
Into the perfectly appointed room
Scorching the hooked rug.
We became brothers—
Of a spiritual kind—
As we began to bind
Up wounds.
You bore my burden,
And I yours
As we did church—
Souls seeking community.
Time and space, and life and death
Have distanced us,
But that moment of compassion
Is still burning bright in my memory.
You were the face of grace to me then
And now.

Mayan Dream

Pushing through the vegetation
Wet with recent rains,
Or tears of a foreign god who laments
Another futile sacrifice to the Golden Sun and the Feathery Serpent.
The sacrifice stumbles, unable to stop his collapse
Falling face first, breaking his nose, cutting his cheek
The blood tastes like the ocean where he played as a
Brown, naked child
Shiny as the reflections that gleam on the smooth, brown, round rocks
On the beach.
He wants to be there again, but that place is in the great cloud palace of
the past
Where his mother and wise old grandfather now live.
He is dragged back to the painful present
As he is yanked to his feet
By the cords that bind his wrist tied behind his back.
A spear goads his side.
A grunt tells him that he must continue to walk through the weeping
trees
To the open expanse surrounding the giant pyr
amid.
Staggering, he climbs the steps of the great temple monument
One tentative foot ahead of the other.
Fear mounts in his heart as cold as the stone steps he ascends
Bringing supplicants nearer to the eternally thirsty Sun.

Feathered ecclesiastical robes—the sacrifice of the jungle birds—
Shimmer in the sunlight like jewels.
An old noble woman kneels
And runs a serrated vine through her tender, protruding tongue
Pouring out her royal blood as another offering
Splattering on her golden ceremonial sandals
Like rubies.
He is stretched across the still warm and slippery altar.
He sees her dabble at her chin to wipe her bloody flow,
Their eyes meet and he sees a vacant narcotic stare,
Eyes of flint.
He sees the sharp glint of the stone knife
As the ecstatic priest holds it high, singing.
He sees the swift descent of muscled arms.
He sees his heart held aloft, still beating.
He feels only sadness, no more fear
As his blood mingles with the countless other offerings
To the universal, voracious, religious passion.
He hears a bird sing.
He goes to the music,
As his blood flows down the stone gutters
Spilled to satisfy ancient urges to reach the unreachable
To know the unknowable.

Sunset

You hang high
In the late afternoon sky.
Skim-milk moon
Like a flawed pearl.
You blanch
As the sun sets
Taillight red
In the amethyst swirl in the rearview mirror
Leaving momentarily
The deep blue Texas sky stained New Mexico purple.

Whispering Hope

Tonight eternity's prelude is played
On helicopter blades.
Hawk Eye swooping down to save her?
Or was it a hawk?
Or was it an angel
In dark flowing robes
With silver stars and crescent moons
Embroidered on swirls of gossamer silks?
I think the latter.
And she scooped up your mother
Out of her confinement,
Leaving a brittle, broken chrysalis behind.
Gently covering her with tender wings,
She brushed away webs of pain and sorrow from around that wounded
spirit.
And as you held her hand, Barb,
She slipped away from you
As easily as a butterfly
Dances past dazzling daffodils,
Delighted to be released.
Eyes opened
Drinking in all the beauty there—
Just in front of her—
Happy to feel her own mother's welcoming kiss.
She left

Not bothering to close the curtains
Because everything was revealed.
There did not have to be any more discreet secrets
In the Promised Land of Light.

Beginning Again

Beginning again with requiem
A somber, holy sound.
A bed of wood
In solemnity
Lowered into the ground.
Sleep in dark,
A waiting time—
A momentary affliction—
Until angels come
Rolling stones
Announcing,
"Resurrection!"

Sun Baptized

You had been abandoned by all—
Even God, it seemed.
Parents, humiliated by your sexual orientation,
Terrified of your Bohemian disease,
Somehow made you not welcome
At home.
Religion, made of rigid rules,
Afraid of your newfound freedom,
Bluntly held you at bay,
Made you not welcome
At home.
My wife, who loved you like music,
Sent me, barely a believer,
Two hundred miles weekly to take you to
AIDS Services.
There those who had not abandoned you,
Filled grocery bags
With food you could not eat,
Offered clean clothes
That did not fit.
Tea and sympathy
Like genial chatter
About T-cell counts,
Legislation,
The latest medication,
Tried to make you a home.

One sunny day,
After our customary lunch in a Thai restaurant
With an ambience that was distinctly non-protestant,
You merely rearranged food on your plate
As demon idols, disguised as part of the décor, glared
Like fiends from Hell.
You asked if we could take a little drive.
"Yes, I'd be glad to," I lied.
We walked across the parking lot
With you fighting against the slightest breeze
As though it were a hurricane.
Your steps were crisp,
Elbows bent,
Wrists relaxed,
Head held high,
And you looked . . .
Not so much queenly
As noble.
Minutes later my automobile
Became your chariot
As I chauffeured you past open fields
Of clipped stubble,
A reminder of cycles,
Rolling fences
Testifying to rusty boundaries;
Common pastoral scenes
Of serene cows,
A remembrance of more innocent times.

You lowered your window
And stuck your head out of the car into the wind.
Smiling,
You gratefully accepted the simple gift of the sun's warmth
On a Texas winter day
In silent delight
Like a gentle benediction.
Your closed eyes,
Your radiant face
Illustrated for me
Communion with our common denominator.
Your reverie
Encouraged my fragile faith
As I realized
You did not feel abandoned,
You felt at home
With me,
And your fate.

I Have Witnessed

I have witnessed
The awesome dignity of primary grief.
I have measured
The unfathomable depths of solitary sorrow.
I have felt
The trembling hand try desperately to touch familiarity
And only touch cold clay.
I have observed
My sight blur through tears because it hurts to see.
And as what I see becomes what I saw
Memory seesaws in my mind
Between a laughing father
And the undertaker's art,
Between light and the gathering dark,
Between life and death,
Between absolute stillness
And an imagined intake
Of my dead father's breath.

Grotesque Buoys

They floated like grotesque buoys
Beneath the circling gulls,
Above the creeping crab's claws
Full as distended balloons
Just before they rupture.
Had they just enjoyed their
Last supper
Unaware of the poison betrayal
Hidden in the bread willing them dead?
In their small scurrying minds
Had they only a few moments to look up at
Each other
In surprise,
And see horror reflected in each other's
Beady eyes
Before the desperate pain
Forced them to rush
And drink gulps
From the salty sea?
They silently marked hidden dangers in the
Water
Just off the shore of Corpus Christi,
Their heads beneath the waves
Bobbing greetings to their watery graves.
Their long, naked tails frozen in death
Stabbed deep into my eyes,
And my breath rushed

Down the beach screaming in terror of rats
And death
While I strolled leisurely along the way
And philosophized about the
Existential truths learned that day.

They Gathered Like Country Guests

They gathered like country guests
To a garden party.
The canopy was stretched and raised
As everyone marveled at the weather
And the sun blazed.
People chatted
Children's heads were patted
And butter-yellow butterflies gadded
About their nervous dance unable to
Rout our fear of death.
They lit on cut flowers artfully arrayed
Trying in vain to conceal
What was all too real.
The guest of honor arrived—
Dignified gentleman.
Words were read
A prayer was said
A sad song was sung.
As the flowers wilted
The guest became stilted
And the polite talk died.
One small woman in her widow's black dress
Turned and ignored the guest,
Bowed her head
Softly cried.

As for man, his days are as grass: as a flower of the field, so he flourisheth. For the wind passeth over it, and it is gone . . . . But the mercy of the LORD is from everlasting to everlasting.

PSALM 103:15-17

Forty Years Ago

Forty years ago you passed your prime,
But you never stopped, you kept on trying
To plow a straight furrow.
A night on the porch, with your feet propped up,
Your stomach full of biscuits and gravy from supper,
You rolled a cigarette and quietly smoked.
Sometimes you thought, sometimes you joked.
What were you thinking about, Grandpa?
Your milky blue eyes kept looking away.
But, somehow, you never had much to say about what you saw.
What did you see out there, Grandpa?
Did you see the past—all those hard years?
Were you looking at the future?
Did that bring those tears so close to the surface?
Or did what you see have anything to do with time?
Thank you, Sir, for the dime.
What did you keep in that old wooden chest?
Gold and silver?
Or was it filled with dreams and hopes and schemes
About building things in the blacksmith shop?
You had strawberry fields before the song.

You hoed them and picked them,
And your life was a long melody
Played on a polished fiddle that hung on a wall
Without any wallpaper—
A solo played high and clear.
What else did you hold dear, besides truth?
There was Grandma, and you loved her for all of those years.
There were thirteen kids and four million tears.
But you laughed, Grandpa, by sucking in all that life;
And letting it rumble around your heart
Then pop out when you slapped your knee.
I loved to watch you laugh, Grandpa,
It made me laugh, too.
You laughed harder than most people.
Was it because things were funnier to you,
Or was it some secret you knew that you kept locked in your old wooden chest?

Like a Wilted Dandelion

Like a wilted dandelion
You barely dent your pillow.
You sleep—
Hands folded—
Like a little girl in prayer.
I brush your hair
And wait
With the others for eternal breath to blow
Soft and gentle
And carry you away with a
Puff.

Forgive Me for Staring

Forgive me for staring.
I know it is rude.
But I hunger to see the light in your eyes.
Please, don't look away.
I hear what you say with your silence.
Since you are the one who goes
And leaves me behind,
I won't think you unkind
If you'll let me look until you go.
I don't know
If I can bear to wait
For forever
To see you again.

There is an appointed time for everything. And there is a time for every event under heaven—A time to give birth, and a time to die.

ECCLESIASTES 3: 1-2

And a Time to Die

Always
On the other side of the window
Is the source of the frost,
A grayness that kisses glass,
Making ice lace.
What is death, anyway?
It is the real thing,
And that's what we want
Isn't it?
Well?
Isn't it?
Screaming red,
Taking big ripping mouthfuls
Of flesh,
Ending all glass games
With one shattering
Halt!

For he himself knows our frame; He is mindful that we are but dust. As for man, his days are like grass; as a flower of the field, so he flourishes. When the wind has passed over it, it is no more; and its place acknowledges it no longer.

PSALM 103:14-16

Heart Song

The sound is low—
Beneath the rumble of the residual roar
Of the first vital moment
Eons ago.
It is beneath silence
And can only be heard when
An ear is pressed to God's chest
As one kneels in adoration.
The rhythm comforts
Like a mother's heart-song to her unborn,
Filling up all available void with
Regular rhythms of being.
That sound is
The basis of our reality—
I Am . . . I Am . . . I Am
A remembered lullaby for the sin-sick soul
Consumed with the longing of an
Ongoing homecoming.

Grief Resurfacing

I tried to recall you,
But when I pressed the button labeled "Mother"
You were not there.
Instead there was
Only a vague feeling of loss,
Of large, soft arms that I wanted to enfold me,
Just a blank where a face should be,
Silence where my mind used to replay your voice
Like a broken record
Calling my name
At unsuspecting times to come to supper,
Or to come home because it was late,
Or simply calling out my name in that beautiful way
That sounded like music to me—
Because you wanted me to answer,
Verifying I was well.
I tried to recall you
And wept again, all these years after the fact,
Because I was never able to thank you,
And tell you how deeply you impacted my life
With notions of beauty.
To see old photographs of you hanging out wash—
Clothespins held by taut lips—
Merely reminds me of your servitude.
Your brave hausfrau poses

Revealed cheery cheeks,
Mahogany hair,
And the light in your eyes mysteriously transferred to mine
Not what you felt or thought—
Rather what should be.
Were you happy manufacturing all those countless biscuits,
Mopping all those acres of floors,
Ironing all those mountains of clothes,
Kissing all those bleeding hurts?
I hope you knew how much you were loved.
I hope this loss of detail of your visage
In my memory
Doesn't diminish you some more.
When I reach out to you now,
There is silence.
Is it because you still have clothespins in your mouth?
Or is it because you are momentarily engaged
In vivacious conversation with Proust and Jung and St. Teresa of Avila?
Oh, God, I hope that it is the latter reason.

It Is Easter Again

It is Easter again
And once more I will have to scrutinize this implausible story
About a corpse rising.
Every year is a test
For me.
Too many hot summer nights in a shanty
Perched on the edge of Tickfaw swamp
Hearing panther's shrill wails
That sound like a terrified woman's screams,
Too many black nights where fear clung closer than
The stifling air,
Closer than a damp, musty shroud,
Made me fearful of the imminent arrival of zombies . . .
The living dead!
They come out of shallow graves in the swamp,
They come out of those old, above-the-ground tombs
In St. Francisville.

If Grandpa Lonnie,
A kind soul who wore a fine Panama straw hat
And a freshly starched
Khaki suit every day of his life,
Were to return from his resting place in that old family cemetery
Where the huge magnolia trees
Grew shinier leaves, and healthier branches,

And larger blooms as pale and waxy as corpses' faces
Because of their bountiful, frightful fertilizer,
It would distress the entire family
Since we expected him to stay there until the final trump sounded.
I, for one, would *not* be glad to see him!
I would scream and run headlong into the night
Down the lane, across the road to Miz Needham's house,
And my hair would be snow white,
And I would have a perpetual twitch.
But every Easter we celebrate
The risen Lord.
I listen to scripture give accounts so rich in wonder
That I weep for the mystery,
And in gratitude for the brave women
Who did not run in terror,
For sweet sister Magdalene
Who stumbled through shimmering curtains of tears
Running into the dawn
Having seen hope reborn,
Faith's assurance,
With courage to tell the incredible truth
That I never have to be afraid again.
And every Easter
I believe a bit more,
Sing a bit louder,
Pray a bit deeper,
And meet with as many people as I can
In order to sing with all the faith I can muster,

"Christ the Lord is risen today,
A-A-Alleluia!"

Eternal Lullaby

I said I would not miss you.
It seemed a silly thing
To bring someone from far away
And hold her in a dream.
And talk to her of sacred things,
Walk with her in the dew
Hear the waves, feel the shore,
And wish that dreams were true.
And, yet, at night you come to me
And often make me weep,
And, so, because I dream of you
I am in love with sleep.

"Let not your heart be troubled; Believe in God, believe also in me. In my Father's house are many dwelling places; if it were not so, I would have told you; for I go to prepare a place for you. And if I go and prepare a place for you, I will come again, and receive you to myself; that where I am, there you may be also."

JOHN 14:1-3

I Saw God Today

I saw God today
Traveling faster than light
Across the cosmos
Away from me.
He was laughing and dancing
Like a child
Pleased with what she had done.
In the wake of this twirling dance
Stars and suns burst into life
Like phosphorous in the midnight blue of the Caribbean
As darkness shivered in anticipation.
Could this be the same one who wanted us
Ignorant, idiot savants,
Drooling as we sang praises parrot-like?
Could this be the same one who wanted us banished
Like screaming banshees
Wailing for Eden's loss,
Waiting to die?
Always death awaited,
Even before we ate of the tree of knowledge.

Always destined to die.
And then, fearful we would live forever,
He severed our umbilical cord
With an angel's flaming sword,
Keeping us forever out.

But the God I saw today
Was full of delight,
And as real as the heavenly monarch
Isaiah saw the year King Uzziah died.
This God was vast,
I was paltry.
Yet I called,
I cried,
I shouted,
I wailed.
But he was too far away, I thought.
Ears too full of the
Primordial roaring of galaxies
To hear me,
Eyes too focused on the dazzle of
Ten thousand galaxies being born
To see me,
Arms too open for dancing with eternity
To hold me.
But I saw that he lives.
Largest of all
And indisputable

Outside all definitions,
Boundaries,
Theologies,
Time,
Space,
The human race.
And I was more finite,
Yet more eternal
Than I ever dared dream,
And more tenacious because
I saw him and tasted him
And it was good,
And engendered more goodness.
And the Creator smiled
And urged me to dance.
"But what if I stumble?"
"We'll make it part of the dance.
And don't fear, I have faith in you!" He laughed,
Opening inclusive arms.
We waltzed.

In the Tomb

In the depths of the silent dark—
There was no echo,
No dim reflection
Like a faint echo of light,
Only an impenetrable black void.
The women stood there looking into the depths
Trembling in terror and grief
Afraid to enter,
When they both saw it.
What is it they saw,
Or hoped,
Or longed to see?
There was a flicker
Of faith,
Of possibility.
Held up against the despairing darkness,
That dim luminosity
Allowed their eyes to adjust to a needle sharp focus.
They saw light in the tomb.
And like a clarion call from Gabriel's own trumpet
It declared:
He is not here.
He is risen.
You do not have to be afraid ever again.
There is life after life.

Some called that glimmer an angel,
And it was.
Some called it a metaphor,
And it was.
Some called it truth,
And it was.
Some called it the good news,
And it was.
Some called it the ultimate message from God.
And it was,
Is
And ever shall be.

Looking Out

Looking out the large window down at
St. Augustine grass, green with photosynthesis,
Looking, looking, looking
For an inspiration.
An answer.
What?
Looking for the evidences of three score and ten years
Well spent
When I was absent
From most of them.
And I see the leaf—
Pine, oak, magnolia—
Then cone and acorn
Making me feel bereft, forlorn
As bright days shift into shade
Like summer passing from golden autumnal equinox
To a black and white winter solstice.
It is death for which I look
Outside the second story window,
Alone, peering from behind the drapes.
Fearful,
Not wanting to broach that taboo subject
Lest I upset the citizenry
With such somber, fearful thoughts.
Why fear?

No surprise, really.
The unknown.
My poor, fading sight,
My waning hearing,
My aching, arthritic shoulders,
My faint memory of passions past,
My rows of bottles of pills that regulate a failing heart
Are small, muted trumpets playing a diminutive fanfare
Announcing something I dread and do not dare
To say aloud.
So like a monk meditating in a cold, sparse cell
On sadness, suffering and cold, winter rain,
Solitude, and rectitude for a soul racked with existential pain,
I journey searching for
The answer
That causes me to stare from my large window,
Looming as real as a potentially ominous winter,
Goading as deeply as a two-thousand-year-old wooden splinter
From the cross of the Christ
Into the palm of my hand
Inexorably reminding of the ever-present promise
Of spring,
And the unanswerable question, "Why?"
And I hear whispered through a barely stifled laugh,
"Why not?"

What's the Word?

It was too late, they told me.
I did not make it.
I did not make it.
I did not make it.
You were already gone,
In spite of the fact that the machine forced your chest up and down
Mechanically.

You loved mechanics:
Fixing cars,
Old broken things,
Young misshapen things.
You sometimes just sat silently as though waiting
For words—yours or mine—
To bridge the gap, the chasm, the void.
They did not come,
They did not come,
They did not come,
But hovered there like gnats
Darting, circling, biting, buzzing
On a hot day in damp Louisiana.
But buzzing gnats never say
What so desperately needs
To be heard.

Was I too late?
I stood over your sheet-shrouded body
Looking down directly into your still handsome face
Heart breaking, mind groping
For words,
And spoke to the corpse,
"Thank you."
Were you still hovering there waiting for me
To say good-bye to you?
I doubt it;
But the buzzing of the insistent gnats . . .
Had stopped.
The chasm was bridged.
The words were said audibly
As silent tears mutely testified to profound paternal love.

Bonhoeffer's Grave

At three thirty the sun was already fading red,
Deepening Berlin's solemn gray to charcoal—
A color well suited for a city with a somber history
As heavy as an old worn, wet, wool overcoat.
His grave is not in a prime location,
And it takes a search to locate it on the last row of the cemetery—
Humble still in death—
Would the last ever be first?
His name chiseled in stone carved
From his tortured fatherland:
BONHOEFFER
The only marking.
We stand by his grave
With brash American enthusiasm—
Victors posing for photographs—
Hurrying against the fading light
Doubting we could ever capture
This bizarre moment or the essence of this pilgrimage,
Pausing to pray in a dark, walled cemetery.
Silence, then spontaneous singing—
"A Mighty Fortress Is Our God."
Passing through the gates,
We re-entered the city
Like contemplative monks in a row
Joining the bustle of Berlin streets

With industrious passers-by
Never noticing our somber countenance that
Testified to a visit to Bonhoeffer's grave.

Buchenwald

A bleak place of death.
Dining on grief and gall
Proved to be a grim repast, acrid,
Not sweet and succulent with redemption and hope
Like bread and wine at the Lord's Supper.
No, bitter as murder,
Salty as tears of orphans
As they eat rocks,
Grinding and breaking teeth.
Sacrament of evil incarnate.
Terror is consumed unable to satiate.
Despair, the after-dinner drink,
The digestif.

Nazis held opponents of their regime:
Gypsies, Jews, Jehovah's Witnesses, homosexual people
And children.
Children used for thousands of experiments
Until experiments failed,
And they were discarded like wadded up cellophane
All crackly and quickly consumed in the ovens.
In the midst of gypsies, Jews, Jehovah's Witnesses, homosexual people
And children,
Was Bonhoeffer breaking rocks?
Did he preach to this ragged congregation of misfits?

Could he comfort them after hope had faded
Like color drained from their gray faces?
In their lice-infected bunks, did they whisper of earlier days
In voices that rustled like dry, dead leaves?
Did Dietrich become the face of Christ
For those who witnessed for Jehovah?
Did he hold the little children like Jesus did
And kiss their shaved heads?
Did their short, bristled hair prick his lips
Like little crowns of thorns?
Did he hold the hand of one wearing a pink triangle,
And embrace that emaciated body like a brother?
Where was God?
Where was Christ?
Where was the Holy Spirit?
Was Divinity there in Bonhoeffer, burning like a flame
For those broken bodies and anemic souls?
When the world was blackest and bleakest,
Was the Incarnation manifested again
Two miles from Weimar
That bleak November day
In an outpost of hell
Called Buchenwald?

Truth Arrived

Truth arrived in a text
Undecipherable to us.
Slowly the dots and dashes
Coalesced into a code of distinguishable patterns,
And death was introduced dramatically
Like a royal suitor being announced
To hopeful maiden ladies,
Like a big-game hunter
To a nervous gathering of gazelles.
You were the first of our merry band
Of music makers
To draw so near to the precipice
Where mortal is transformed into immortality.
Tears and speechless silence punctuated
The scene we were called on to play.
You, true to your script,
Talked on and on about
You:
"My color's good."
Silence.
"I've gained some weight."
Silence.
"My skin's clearing up."
Silence.
"My color's good."

Silence.

"I can't believe this!"

Silence.

"My eyes are swollen."

Silence.

"My color's good."

I listened to your denial,

Helpless to comfort you, my dear friend.

Unable to chart with you

The map that reveals

Your destination.

We didn't know if it was the beginning of your journey,

Or the end.

It's a Funeral Day

It's a funeral day,
Gray,
Somber,
Serious.
The windows are closed.
The silence has imposed
Stillness on my heart,
And I mourn for dead dreams.

Yesterday's Pains

Yesterday's pains fall like tomorrow's rains
Cold and lonely.
Yesterday's dreams come like tomorrow's hope
Gone or broken.
Yesterday and tomorrow are the same day,
Both start the same way,
Without you.
Now is all I can stand.
Don't let tomorrow come.
Don't let tomorrow come.
Don't let tomorrow come
Without you.

More Questions

How high is high?
Every time I try
To find out
It sets me off
On a string of thoughts about:
God,
And Mind,
And Life.
Why is there strife?

How lovely is love?
Why do we shove
And look for it
In strange places
In new faces and things like:
A new car,
Cuban cigars,
Martin guitars?
How many stars?

What good is gold?
How long is now?
Could it ever be
Anything else but,
Except when it's gone

Into a short list of times like:
> The Past,
> The Future,
> Or Eternity?
> How can that be?

Visitation

It is cold,
Silver and gray.
I flew away today
Through the mist
Over the woods
To see you,
But I couldn't find you.
You were not at home.

How much higher
Must I fly
Before I die
Like Daedalus
With my carefully crafted wings
Melted?

Where Are You Wandering?

Where are you wandering?
Why are you leisurely strolling slowly without a sound
In your embroidered gown
Over acres of reflective onyx
Through innocent light
On holy nights?
Where are you?
Can't I be there, too?
I'm tired of blue jeans
Lifeless music making machines
And endless theatrical scenes
With glaring slivers of intenseness that reveals
Nothing.
I want to play with the happy, laughing children
And share their joy.
I want to walk on purple sand
On a timeless shore
Be a little boy again;
And, yet, be a man some more.
Please!
I'm tired of concrete and smoke,
Vanilla ice cream and Coke,
Seeing life as some sort of meaningless
Existential joke.
Where are you?
Why can't I be there, too?

And the Darkness Can Never Conquer

Through all the games and light
Expressed in clouds, shadows and prisms,
Through all the color and merry fragments
Of bell-shaped Tiffany lamps
There remains
The lead-gray solder
Holding all those deep-throated reds,
Bright cheery golds,
Cool, watery blues
Together.
Death makes a net,
But light sometimes escapes.

Resurrection Morning

Standing alone in a hotel room
I could not imagine who stabbed me,
But a wicked dagger pierced me,
Pressed into my sternum by a strong spectral force.
Instinctively my hand clutched my heart,
I gasped, "God!"
A reflex or a prayer?
It did not matter
As every breath had me reciting a litany of,
"Oh, God! . . . Oh, God! . . . Oh, God! . . ."
I knew it was a heart attack,
The big one!
I managed to phone a friend,
Stagger to the door and unlock it,
Make it to a chair and continue the mantra of all those who fear death
"Oh, God! . . . Oh, God! . . . Oh, God! . . ."
There was no time to wait, as time was not relevant.
The EMS read my sweating, blanched face
And started their work
Thereby joining in my prayer of,
"Oh, God! . . . Oh, God! . . . Oh, God! . . ."

Sirens, horns, speed, prayer unrelenting, agonizing pain
Accompanied the frantic drive to the hospital.
During that Now, I was aware of another person in the ambulance,
Just over my left shoulder

A familiar person, a person I would have wanted by me during this
Life and death transition.
"Daddy?" I called out. "Daddy?"
Only the siren answered loud as a trumpet.
We arrived.
Noise, shouts, running, ceilings whizzing past.
"On a scale of one to ten, what is your pain?"
TEN!

Then silence.
The Now had transitioned into that dimension
Where Sound had not followed,
Nor Pain.
"Good," I thought as I looked down on my body
With someone compressing my chest.
"Hmmm, if I am up here in the corner of the ceiling looking down at me,
I must be in trouble.
Well, I am still thinking, so I'm not dead, am I?
Am I?"
The Presence that had traveled with me in the ambulance
Continued to hover by my left shoulder
So I turned to look
And saw nothing . . . no thing,
The essence of what was observed when the Veil of the Temple
Was ripped from top to bottom.
No thing,
The essence of what was revealed in the empty Tomb,
No thing.

"If I die," I thought, "I'll go be with God and Mamma and Daddy and Jesus.
If I live, I'll be with Cynthia and Will and Lily.
It is a win/win situation!"
And whoever or whatever I was up there floating in the corner of that ceiling laughed.

Rest, quiet. Who knows for how long,
But I heard a voice calling,
"Mr. Courtney . . . Mr. Courtney?"
I opened my eyes to a smiling face.
"Hello. We lost you for a bit. You have had what we call 'the widow maker,'
But you are going to be OK."

I knew.
And the next morning, Easter morning
I woke up to a renewed faith.
"So this is what Lazarus felt like!"

"It was not Daddy in the ambulance with me. It was You.
And Daddy, since he is in You and You are in him,
And he is in me, and I am in him,
And because we love,
We are in You
Because You are love."
I laughed in the morning light streaming into the hospital window
Welcoming Resurrection Morning!

Maya Angelou

She was a trumpet,
A black trumpet.
No, there are no black trumpets.
There are brass trumpets,
But she was not brass.
She had all the twists and bends
Of a brass trumpet, and something of that sound,
But she was not brass,
You can bet your sweet ass!
She was pure gold.
And the music that poured from that large, laughing mouth
Made us all laugh,
Or sing,
Or want to sing.
Here's the thing:
She turned ignorance into wisdom,
Suffering into her great reward,
Persecution into the Kingdom of God.
As she exits this place,
Her song fades as she ascends,
Leaving us all, her friends,
Remembering her lovely music,
Inspiring us as we follow
Not too far behind.
Wasn't she kind
To remind us of truth?

One Year Later
(Or a Lifetime)

On the road to Glorieta,
New Mexican sun warm,
Giving a more radiant light,
Revealing a crisper sight,
Illuminating memories as numerous
As erect needles in forests of pines
When holy times
Were expressed in sacred rhymes
And music
As we sang and slowly swayed
Coming as close to dancing to familiar hymns
And newly birthed anthems
As our rigid religion would allow.

In the warm wash of recollections there appears:
A raw realization,
A clash of times,
A stunning jolt.
A shattering of my fragile mind.
Like a bolt from the blue
Comes a fact feeling like an ancient dread,
And I sigh,
"Buryl Red is dead."

Mother Emanuel Church

This is heavy.
It feels like cold gray lead enclosing my heart,
A thick metal box
Closing in the dark.
It feels like the weight of a large slab of cold Carrara marble
Lying on the dirt of a freshly dug grave
Not yet a noble memorial.
Closed eyes hold back the tears
As the heart beats like a slow funeral drum.
And Death in long black robes
Moans in distress
For the ones he has come to lead home,
Groans in regret for the calling he answers
That leads souls from here to there.
He whispers, almost apologetically, their names:
"Clementa Pinckney,
Cynthia Hurd,
Tywanza Sanders,
Myra Thompson,
Ethel Lance,
Suzie Jackson,
DePayne Middleton-Doctor,
Sharondra Coleman-Singleton,
Daniel Simmons.
Ya'll come on home now,

You hear.

I know this was sudden,

But I was always near

Not as an enemy but as a friend,

And I tell you, sweet martyrs

This is not the end."

And so in our sorrow and deep sense of grief

We call out to God for some sign of relief

And in that sorrow pouring out like lamentations in our collective voice

Resurrection reminds us that

Because of their lives we will finally rejoice.

Last Will and Testament

I started another trip this morning
And concern for my children
Whispered a warning in my ear:
"After so many flights, so many miles on the road
Chances are increasing each time
That this time
Could be the last time."
I wrote a hasty Last Will and Testament
Leaving to them things I had collected
Feeling a bit inadequate tidying up loose ends at the last minute.
I mentioned insurance policies,
And royalties,
Guardians,
Grandparents,
And a nurturing home
All the necessary things
A Last Will and Testament brings.
In my fantasy I tried to be brave
With thoughts of me and my wife in
An adjoining grave.

High over Santa Fe
I remembered all the things I forgot
To will to our children, so I started at the top.
A lifetime filled with each kaleidoscope season,
The joy of figuring out a problem using reason,

The taste of water in a cool mountain stream,
The exhilaration available to dream a dream,
The courage to walk barefoot in a summer
Pasture filled with stickers,
The fun of picking blackberries
When laughing cousins are the pickers,
The pride of fixing a broken toy,
Secret handshakes with a neighborhood boy,
Intoxicating first love that makes us feel dizzy,
The thrill of a full day that keeps us busy,
Then sunshine,] some laughter then a little pain
Laughter, Lord, and the right amount of rain.

If we are not there tomorrow
Comfort them, Lord, they are too small to learn sorrow.
Help them grow wise and tall
Let them know we loved them most of all.

The Death of the Good Reverend

It was heavier than I remembered,
This thing called Death.
It appeared at the onset of dawn
As it's victim—
No, client—
No, customer—
No, charge—
No, ward—
Curled up like a young boy
In an old reclining chair
As soft, worn and cradling
As his mother's strong, young arms were
Ninety-one years ago.
In the soft whispered light
He rested his tired old head
On his spotted hand,
Closed his eyes
Too tired to open them ever again,
Too tired to call out to his precious daughter
Listening in the next room,
Too tired to acknowledge the cold
Creeping over his limbs,
Too tired to register that new, bright light
Radiating through his this eye lids,
Too tired to smile any larger,

Or respond
As he heard the singing getting closer,
Too tired to respond to the embrace
Of stronger arms around him.
He merely lay there resting,
Feeling peace.
Now he could take his own sweet time to open his eyes.

"Let not your heart be troubled; Believe in God, believe also in me. In my Father's house are many dwelling places; if it were not so I would have told you; for I go to prepare a place for you. And if I go and prepare a place for you, I will come again, and receive you to myself; that where I am, there you may be also."

JOHN 14

Hope Eternal

Thank God for John 14.
It is like a bud of green
During this winter.
A promise,
A hope
When you are at the end
Unable to grope
For fear of what cold thing
You will touch
In the dark,
There is a spark.
Thank God for John 14.

Other available titles from SMYTH&HELWYS

#Connect
Reaching Youth Across the Digital Divide
Brian Foreman

Reaching our youth across the digital divide is a struggle for parents, ministers, and other adults who work with Generation Z—today's teenagers. #Connect leads readers into the technological landscape, encourages conversations with teenagers, and reminds us all to be the presence of Christ in every facet of our lives. 978-1-57312-693-9 120 pages/pb **$13.00**

Beginnings
A Reverend and a Rabbi Talk About the Stories of Genesis
Michael Smith and Rami Shapiro

Editor Aaron Herschel Shapiro declares that stories "must be retold—not just repeated, but reinvented, reimagined, and reexperienced" to remain vital in the world. Mike and Rami continue their conversations from the *Mount and Mountain* books, exploring the places where their traditions intersect and diverge, listening to each other as they respond to the stories of Genesis. 978-1-57312-772-1 202 pages/pb **$18.00**

Choosing Gratitude
Learning to Love the Life You Have
James A. Autry

Autry reminds us that gratitude is a choice, a spiritual—not social—process. He suggests that if we cultivate gratitude as a way of being, we may not change the world and its ills, but we can change our response to the world. If we fill our lives with moments of gratitude, we will indeed love the life we have. 978-1-57312-614-4 144 pages/pb **$15.00**

Choosing Gratitude 365 Days a Year
Your Daily Guide to Grateful Living
James A. Autry and Sally J. Pederson

Filled with quotes, poems, and the inspired voices of both Pederson and Autry, in a society consumed by fears of not having "enough"—money, possessions, security, and so on—this book suggests that if we cultivate gratitude as a way of being, we may not change the world and its ills, but we can change our response to the world. 978-1-57312-689-2 210 pages/pb **$18.00**

To order call **1-800-747-3016** or visit **www.helwys.com**

Crisis Ministry: A Handbook
Daniel G. Bagby

Covering more than 25 crisis pastoral care situations, this book provides a brief, practical guide for church leaders and other caregivers responding to stressful situations in the lives of parishioners. It tells how to resource caregiving professionals in the community who can help people in distress. 978-1-57312-370-9 *154 pages/pb* **$15.00**

Crossroads in Christian Growth
W. Loyd Allen

Authentic Christian life presents spiritual crises and we struggle to find a hero walking with God at a crossroads. With wisdom and sincerity, W. Loyd Allen presents Jesus as our example and these crises as stages in the journey of growth we each take toward maturity in Christ. 978-1-57312-753-0 *164 pages/pb* **$15.00**

A Divine Duet
Ministry and Motherhood
Alicia Davis Porterfield, ed.

Each essay in this inspiring collection is as different as the mother-minister who wrote it, from theologians to chaplains, inner-city ministers to rural-poverty ministers, youth pastors to preachers, mothers who have adopted, birthed, and done both. 978-1-57312-676-2 *146 pages/pb* **$16.00**

The Exile and Beyond (All the Bible series)
Wayne Ballard

The Exile and Beyond brings to life the sacred literature of Israel and Judah that comprises the exilic and postexilic communities of faith. It covers Ezekiel, Isaiah, Haggai, Zechariah, Malachi, 1 & 2 Chronicles, Ezra, Nehemiah, Joel, Jonah, Song of Songs, Esther, and Daniel. 978-1-57312-759-2 *196 pages/pb* **$16.00**

Fierce Love
Desperate Measures for Desperate Times
Jeanie Miley

Fierce Love is about learning to see yourself and know yourself as a conduit of love, operating from a full heart instead of trying to find someone to whom you can hook up your emotional hose and fill up your empty heart. 978-1-57312-810-0 *276 pages/pb* **$18.00**

To order call **1-800-747-3016** or visit **www.helwys.com**

Five Hundred Miles
Reflections on Calling and Pilgrimage
Lauren Brewer Bass

Spain's Camino de Santiago, the Way of St. James, has been a cherished pilgrimage path for centuries, visited by countless people searching for healing, solace, purpose, and hope. These stories from her five-hundred-mile-walk is Lauren Brewer Bass's honest look at the often winding, always surprising journey of a calling.   978-1-57312-812-4 *142 pages/pb* **$16.00**

Galatians (Smyth & Helwys Bible Commentary)
Marion L. Soards and Darrell J. Pursiful

In Galatians, Paul endeavored to prevent the Gentile converts from embracing a version of the gospel that insisted on their observance of a form of the Mosaic Law. He saw with a unique clarity that such a message reduced the crucified Christ to being a mere agent of the Law. For Paul, the gospel of Jesus Christ alone, and him crucified, had no place in it for the claim that Law-observance was necessary for believers to experience the power of God's grace.   978-1-57312-771-4 *384 pages/hc* **$55.00**

Glimpses from State Street
Wayne Ballard

As a collection of devotionals, *Glimpses from State Street* provides a wealth of insights and new ways to consider and develop our fellowship with Christ. It also serves as a window into the relationship between a small town pastor and a welcoming congregation.

978-1-57312-841-4 *158 pages/pb* **$15.00**

God's Servants, the Prophets
Bryan Bibb

God's Servants, the Prophets covers the Israelite and Judean prophetic literature from the preexilic period. It includes Amos, Hosea, Isaiah, Micah, Zephaniah, Nahum, Habakkuk, Jeremiah, and Obadiah.

978-1-57312-758-5 *208 pages/pb* **$16.00**

Gray Matters
100 Devotions for the Aging
Edwin Ray Frazier

"Each line rests on Frazier's fundamental belief that every season in life is valuable and rich with opportunity."
—Alicia Davis Porterfield
Interim pastor and former eldercare chaplain

978-1-57312-837-7 *246 pages/pb* **$18.00**

To order call 1-800-747-3016 or visit www.helwys.com

Hermeneutics of Hymnody
A Comprehensive and Integrated Approach to Understanding Hymns
Scotty Gray

Scotty Gray's *Hermeneutics of Hymnody* is a comprehensive and integrated approach to understanding hymns. It is unique in its holistic and interrelated exploration of seven of the broad facets of this most basic forms of Christian literature. A chapter is devoted to each and relates that facet to all of the others.
978-157312-767-7   *432 pages/pb*   **$28.00**

If Jesus Isn't the Answer . . . He Sure Asks the Right Questions!
J. Daniel Day

Taking eleven of Jesus' questions as its core, Day invites readers into their own conversation with Jesus. Equal parts testimony, theological instruction, pastoral counseling, and autobiography, the book is ultimately an invitation to honest Christian discipleship.
978-1-57312-797-4   *148 pages/pb*   **$16.00**

I'm Trying to Lead . . . Is Anybody Following?
The Challenge of Congregational Leadership in the Postmodern World
Charles B. Bugg

Bugg provides us with a view of leadership that has theological integrity, honors the diversity of church members, and reinforces the brave hearts of church leaders who offer vision and take risks in the service of Christ and the church.
978-1-57312-731-8   *136 pages/pb*   **$13.00**

James M. Dunn and Soul Freedom
Aaron Douglas Weaver

James Milton Dunn, over the last fifty years, has been the most aggressive Baptist proponent for religious liberty in the US. Soul freedom—voluntary, uncoerced faith and an unfettered individual conscience before God—is the basis of his understanding of church-state separation and the historic Baptist basis of religious liberty.
978-1-57312-590-1   *224 pages/pb*   **$18.00**

Judaism
A Brief Guide to Faith and Practice
Sharon Pace

Sharon Pace's newest book is a sensitive and comprehensive introduction to Judaism. How does belief in the One God and a universal morality shape the way in which Jews see the world? How does one find meaning in life and the courage to endure suffering? How does one mark joy and forge community ties?
978-1-57312-644-1   *144 pages/pb*   **$16.00**

To order call 1-800-747-3016 or visit www.helwys.com

Luke (Smyth & Helwys Annual Bible Study series)
Parables for the Journey
Michael L. Ruffin

These stories in Luke's Gospel are pilgrimage parables. They are parables for those on the way to being the people of God. They are not places where we stop and stay; they are rather places where we learn what we need to learn and from which, equipped with Jesus' directions, we continue the journey. But we will see that they are also places to which we repeatedly return.
Teaching Guide 978-1-57312-849-0 146 pages/pb **$14.00**
Study Guide 978-1-57312-850-6 108 pages/pb **$6.00**

Meditations on Mark
Daily Devotions from the Oldest Gospel
Chris Cadenhead

Readers searching for a fresh encounter with Scripture can delve into *Meditations on Mark*, a collection of daily devotions intended to guide the reader through the book of Mark, the Oldest Gospel and the first known effort to summarize and proclaim the life and ministry of Jesus.
978-1-57312-851-3 158 pages/pb **$15.00**

Meeting Jesus Today
For the Cautious, the Curious, and the Committed
Jeanie Miley

Meeting Jesus Today, ideal for both individual study and small groups, is intended to be used as a workbook. It is designed to move readers from studying the Scriptures and ideas within the chapters to recording their journey with the Living Christ.
978-1-57312-677-9 320 pages/pb **$19.00**

The Ministry Life
101 Tips for New Ministers
John Killinger

Sharing years of wisdom from more than fifty years in ministry and teaching, *The Ministry Life: 101 Tips for New Ministers* by John Killinger is filled with practical advice and wisdom for a minister's day-to-day tasks as well as advice on intellectual and spiritual habits to keep ministers of any age healthy and fulfilled.
978-1-57312-662-5 244 pages/pb **$19.00**

To order call **1-800-747-3016** or visit **www.helwys.com**

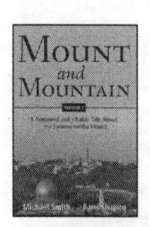

Mount and Mountain
Vol. 2: A Reverend and a Rabbi Talk About the Sermon on the Mount
Rami Shapiro and Michael Smith

This book, focused on the Sermon on the Mount, represents the second half of Mike and Rami's dialogue. In it, Mike and Rami explore the text of Jesus' sermon cooperatively, contributing perspectives drawn from their lives and religious traditions and seeking moments of illumination.

978-1-57312-654-0 *254 pages/pb* **$19.00**

Of Mice and Ministers
Musings and Conversations About Life, Death, Grace, and Everything
Bert Montgomery

With stories about pains, joys, and everyday life, *Of Mice and Ministers* finds Jesus in some unlikely places and challenges us to do the same. From tattooed women ministers to saying the "N"-word to the brotherly kiss, Bert Montgomery takes seriously the lesson from Psalm 139—where can one go that God is not already there?

978-1-57312-733-2 *154 pages/pb* **$14.00**

Place Value
The Journey to Where You Are
Katie Sciba

Does a place have value? Can a place change us? Is it possible for God to use the place you are in to form you? From Victoria, Texas to Indonesia, Belize, Australia, and beyond, Katie Sciba's wanderlust serves as a framework to understand your own places of deep emotion and how God may have been weaving redemption around you all along.

978-157312-829-2 *138 pages/pb* **$15.00**

Reading Joshua
(Reading the Old Testament series)
A Historical-Critical/Archaeological Commentary
John C. H. Laughlin

Using the best of current historical-critical studies by mainstream biblical scholars, and the most recent archaeological discoveries and theorizing, Laughlin questions both the historicity of the stories presented in the book as well as the basic theological ideology presented through these stories: namely that Yahweh ordered the indiscriminate butchery of the Canaanites.

978-1-57312-836-0 *274 pages/pb* **$32.00**

To order call **1-800-747-3016** or visit **www.helwys.com**

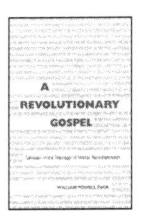

A Revolutionary Gospel
Salvation in the Theology of Walter Rauschenbusch
William Powell Tuck

William Powell Tuck describes how Rauschenbusch's concept of redemption requires a transformation of society as well as individuals—and that no one can genuinely be redeemed without this redemption affecting the social culture as well. *A Revolutionary Gospel* shows us how Rauschenbusch's revolutionary concept of salvation is still relevant today.

978-1-57312-804-9 190 pages/pb **$21.00**

Reflective Faith
A Theological Toolbox for Women
Susan M. Shaw

In *Reflective Faith*, Susan Shaw offers a set of tools to explore difficult issues of biblical interpretation, theology, church history, and ethics—especially as they relate to women. Reflective faith invites intellectual struggle and embraces the unknown; it is a way of discipleship, a way to love God with your mind, as well as your heart, your soul, and your strength.

978-1-57312-719-6 292 pages/pb **$24.00**
Workbook 978-1-57312-754-7 164 pages/pb **$12.00**

Sessions with Ephesians
(Sessions Bible Studies series)
Toward a New Identity in Christ
William L. Self & Michael D. McCullar

Ephesians has been called "the most contemporary book in the Bible." Strip it of just a few first-century references and it would be easily applicable to the modern church.

978-1-57312-838-4 110 pages/pb **$14.00**

Sessions with Psalms (Sessions Bible Studies series)
Prayers for All Seasons
Eric and Alicia D. Porterfield

Useful to seminar leaders during preparation and group discussion, as well as in individual Bible study, *Sessions with Psalms* is a ten-session study designed to explore what it looks like for the words of the psalms to become the words of our prayers. Each session is followed by a thought-provoking page of questions.

978-1-57312-768-4 136 pages/pb **$14.00**

To order call **1-800-747-3016** or visit **www.helwys.com**

Tell the Truth, Shame the Devil
Stories about the Challenges of Young Pastors
James Elllis III, ed.

A pastor's life is uniquely difficult. *Tell the Truth, Shame the Devil*, then, is an attempt to expose some of the challenges that young clergy often face. While not exhaustive, this collection of essays is a superbly compelling and diverse introduction to how tough being a pastor under the age of thirty-five can be.   978-1-57312-839-1 198 pages/pb **$18.00**

Though the Darkness Gather Round
Devotions about Infertility, Miscarriage, and Infant Loss
Mary Elizabeth Hill Hanchey and Erin McClain, eds.

Much courage is required to weather the long grief of infertility and the sudden grief of miscarriage and infant loss. This collection of devotions by men and women, ministers, chaplains, and lay leaders who can speak of such sorrow, is a much-needed resource and precious gift for families on this journey and the faith communities that walk beside them.

978-1-57312-811-7 180 pages/pb **$19.00**

Time for Supper
Invitations to Christ's Table
Brett Younger

Some scholars suggest that every meal in literature is a communion scene. Could every meal in the Bible be a communion text? Could every passage be an invitation to God's grace? These meditations on the Lord's Supper help us listen to the myriad of ways God invites us to gratefully, reverently, and joyfully share the cup of Christ.   978-1-57312-720-2 246 pages/pb **$18.00**

A Time to Laugh
Humor in the Bible
Mark E. Biddle

With characteristic liveliness, Mark E. Biddle explores the ways humor was intentionally incorporated into Scripture. Drawing on Biddle's command of Hebrew language and cultural subtleties, *A Time to Laugh* guides the reader through the stories of six biblical characters who did rather unexpected things.   978-1-57312-683-0 164 pages/pb **$14.00**

To order call **1-800-747-3016** or visit www.helwys.com

A True Hope
Jedi Perils and the Way of Jesus
Joshua Hays

Star Wars offers an accessible starting point for considering substantive issues of faith, philosophy, and ethics. In *A True Hope*, Joshua Hays explores some of these challenging ideas through the sayings of the Jedi Masters, examining the ways the worldview of the Jedi is at odds with that of the Bible. 978-1-57312-770-7 *186 pages/pb* **$18.00**

Word of God Across the Ages
Using Christian History in Preaching
Bill J. Leonard

In this third, enlarged edition, Bill J. Leonard returns to the roots of the Christian story to find in the lives of our faithful forebears examples of the potent presence of the gospel. Through these stories, those who preach today will be challenged and inspired as they pursue the divine Word in human history through the ages. 978-1-57312-828-5 *174 pages/pb* **$19.00**

The World Is Waiting for You
Celebrating the 50th Ordination Anniversary of Addie Davis
Pamela R. Durso & LeAnn Gunter Johns, eds.

Hope for the church and the world is alive and well in the words of these gifted women. Keen insight, delightful observations, profound courage, and a gift for communicating the good news are woven throughout these sermons. The Spirit so evident in Addie's calling clearly continues in her legacy. 978-1-57312-732-5 *224 pages/pb* **$18.00**

With Us in the Wilderness
Finding God's Story in Our Lives
Laura A. Barclay

What stories compose your spiritual biography? In *With Us in the Wilderness*, Laura Barclay shares her own stories of the intersection of the divine and the everyday, guiding readers toward identifying and embracing God's presence in their own narratives.
978-1-57312-721-9 *120 pages/pb* **$13.00**

To order call **1-800-747-3016** or visit **www.helwys.com**

Clarence Jordan's
Cotton Patch Gospel

The Complete Collection

Hardback • 448 pages
Retail ~~50.00~~ • Your Price 25.00

Paperback • 448 pages
Retail ~~40.00~~ • Your Price 20.00

The Cotton Patch Gospel, by Koinonia Farm founder Clarence Jordan, recasts the stories of Jesus and the letters of the New Testament into the language and culture of the mid-twentieth-century South. Born out of the civil rights struggle, these now-classic translations of much of the New Testament bring the far-away places of Scripture closer to home: Gainesville, Selma, Birmingham, Atlanta, Washington D.C.

More than a translation, *The Cotton Patch Gospel* continues to make clear the startling relevance of Scripture for today. Now for the first time collected in a single, hardcover volume, this edition comes complete with a new Introduction by President Jimmy Carter, a Foreword by Will D. Campbell, and an Afterword by Tony Campolo. Smyth & Helwys Publishing is proud to help reintroduce these seminal works of Clarence Jordan to a new generation of believers, in an edition that can be passed down to generations still to come.

SMYTH & HELWYS
To order call **1-800-747-3016**
or visit **www.helwys.com**